JAMES
A DOUBLE-EDGED
BIBLE STUDY

jms
—

JAMES
A DOUBLE-EDGED
BIBLE STUDY

TH1NK LifeChange

TH1NK, an
Imprint of
NavPress

Discipleship Inside Out®

NavPress is the publishing ministry of The Navigators, an international Christian organization and leader in personal spiritual development. NavPress is committed to helping people grow spiritually and enjoy lives of meaning and hope through personal and group resources that are biblically rooted, culturally relevant, and highly practical.

For a free catalog go to www.NavPress.com
or call 1.800.366.7788 in the United States or 1.800.839.4769 in Canada.

contents

introduction
to TH1NK
LifeChange

Double-Edged and Ready for Action

For the word of God is living and active. Sharper than any double-edged sword, it penetrates even to dividing soul and spirit, joints and marrow; it judges the thoughts and attitudes of the heart.

Hebrews 4:12

a reason to study

Studying the Bible is more than homework. It is more than reading a textbook. And it is more than an opportunity for a social gathering. Like Hebrews suggests, the Bible knows us, challenges us, and yes, judges us. Like a double-edged sword, it's sharp enough to cut through our layers of insecurity and pretense to change our lives forever.

Deep down, isn't that what we want–to actually *experience* God's power in our lives, through Scripture? That's what TH1NK LifeChange is all about. The purpose of this Bible study is to connect you intimately with God's Word. It can change you, not only intellectually, but also spiritually, emotionally, maybe even physically. God's Word is that powerful.

The psalmist wrote,

> *What you say goes, GOD,*
> *and stays, as permanent as the heavens.*
> *Your truth never goes out of fashion;*
> *it's as up-to-date as the earth when the sun comes*
> *up. . . .*
> *If your revelation hadn't delighted me so,*
> *I would have given up when the hard times came.*
> *But I'll never forget the advice you gave me;*
> *you saved my life with those wise words.*
> *Save me! I'm all yours.*
> *I look high and low for your words of*
> *wisdom.*
> *The wicked lie in ambush to destroy me,*
> *but I'm only concerned with your plans for me.*
> *I see the limits to everything human,*
> *but the horizons can't contain your commands!*

(PSALM 119:89-90,92-96, MSG)

Do you notice the intimate connection the psalmist has with God *because* of the greatness of the Word? He trusts God, he loves Him, and his greatest desire is to obey. But the only way he knows how to do any of this is by knowing God's voice, God's words.

the details

Each TH1NK LifeChange study covers one book of the Bible so you can concentrate on its particular, essential details. Although every study exclusively covers a different book, there are common threads throughout the series. Each study will:

1. Help you understand the book you're studying so well that it affects your daily thinking
2. Teach valuable Bible study skills you can use on your own to go even deeper into God's Word
3. Provide a contextual understanding of the book, offering historical background, word definitions, and explanatory notes
4. Allow you to understand the message of the book as a whole
5. Demonstrate how God's Word can transform you into an authentic representative of Jesus

Every week, plan on spending thirty to forty-five minutes on your own to complete the study. Then get together with your group. Depending on the amount of time it takes, you can go through either a whole or half lesson each week. If you do one lesson per week, you'll finish the study in three months. It's all up to you.

the structure

The twelve lessons include the following elements:

Study. First you'll study the book by yourself. This is where you'll answer questions, learn cultural and biographical information, and ask God some questions of your own.

Live. After you've absorbed the information, you'll want to look in a mirror – figuratively, that is. Think about your life in the context of what you learned. This is a time to be honest with yourself and with God about who you are and how you are living.

Connect. You know that a small-group study time isn't just for hanging out and drinking soda. A small group provides account-ability and support. It's one thing to say to yourself, *I'm really going to work on this* and entirely another thing to say it to a group of friends. Your friends can support your decisions, encourage you to follow through, and pray for you regularly. And vice versa.

In your group, you'll want to talk with each other about what you discovered on your own: things that went unanswered, things that challenged you, and things that changed you. Use the guidance in this section to lead your discussion. After that, pray for each other. This section will always provide targeted prayer topics for you and your group.

Go Deeper. Thirsty for more? Just can't get enough? Then use the guidance in this section to explore more deeply the vastness of Scripture. It's similar to extra credit, for all the overachievers who love to learn.

Memory Verse of the Week. Did a particular verse make you think? Is there a verse you can't get out of your head? Write it down and memorize it. Allow God's Word to permanently brand itself in your head and your heart.

Notes from Group Discussion. At the end of each chapter, there is space for notes. Use it to write notes from your group discussions, to ask questions of God or yourself, to write important verses and observations, or for anything else you want to jot down.

now go!

You are now ready to experience God and the Bible in an intense new way. So jump in headfirst. Allow the double-edged sword of Scripture to pierce your mind, your heart, your life.

faith in action

Ah, good intentions. We intend to clean our rooms—actually we hope to keep our rooms clean in the first place—but that almost never happens. We intend to get homework done early, or at least on time, but slacking off gets the best of us. We intend to work out three times a week, but ohhh, enjoying those cheeseburgers, fries, and shakes looks like a much better way to spend our time.

In the same way, we intend to make godly decisions and live godly lives, *we really do,* but so many things get in the way: distractions, lack of discipline, lack of knowledge . . . the list goes on and on.

Seems like good intentions just don't cut it. What good are good intentions and nice words if we don't carry them through? James presents and answers this question. His book is a commentary on faith and wisdom in action. "Do not merely listen to the word, and so deceive yourselves," he says. "Do what it says. Anyone who listens to the word but does not do what it says is like a man who looks at his face in a mirror and, after looking at himself, goes away and immediately forgets what he looks like" (1:22-24).

James' letter to the church provides practical advice on

how to act on our good intentions. By studying his God-inspired letter, we can develop a deeper motivation to live in pursuit of wisdom and godliness.

Before we dive in, let's look at some biographical, cultural, and historical information about the book of James.

who was James?

In biblical times, there were a lot of men named James. (Kind of like today, really.) It's uncertain which of the many Jameses wrote this book. Tradition leads us to believe that the most likely candidate was James, the brother of Jesus. He was probably the oldest of Jesus' four younger brothers.

James didn't always believe in his brother. It wasn't until Jesus rose again that James fully appreciated Him. Before this deity-solidifying event, James and the rest of his family thought Jesus was a little crazy, constantly wandering through Galilee and Judea proclaiming some "kingdom of God." *(Wasn't this the same guy that used to wrestle him down, play pranks, and do all the other stuff brothers usually do?)* But once James understood his brother, he became a leader in the church himself–Paul even called him one of the pillars of the church. He was with Peter when Paul visited three years after his conversion; he was the person Peter contacted after miraculously escaping from prison; and he provided a convincing argument to the council in Jerusalem, challenging them to accept Gentiles into God's family.

James was called "the Just" or "the Righteous" by Christians and non-Christians alike. Early leaders in the church sometimes claimed that James was called those things because he was somewhat of a perfectionist when it came to observing the law. On the other hand, a Jewish historian wrote in AD 62 that James was killed after somehow *violating* the law. Either way, we know that James was committed to making the gospel accessible to the Gentiles, claiming that the law was not necessary for salvation. He suggested a compromise to deal with the specifics of the law on less important matters, such as what foods Christians were allowed to eat.

history

Scholars still debate about when James was written. Some say he wrote this letter in AD 45, which would mean James is the earliest New Testament book. If this is the case, James' purpose was to challenge Christians to take a good, hard look at their lives and make the changes necessary to live for God—through faith *and* action.

Others suggest James was written around AD 55 to 60. They believe this primarily because of its relationship—or better, its contrast—to Paul's letters. Paul's teachings were a popular conversation piece in early Christian society and were often misquoted and misconstrued. Many people figured that, because salvation was available whether or not they obeyed the law, they could disregard God's moral law entirely. James' letter may have been a response to the misunderstanding of Paul's words.

copycat?

When Martin Luther put together his version of the New Testament in 1522, he decided the books of James, Hebrews, Jude, and Revelation were only supplemental to the rest of the Bible. He didn't think there was enough "gospel character" in James and deemed it "strawy" (Luther-speak for "trivial"). On top of that, James hardly mentioned Jesus at all, and he never wrote anything about His death and resurrection, which also made some early believers leery of his book.

But this controversy is easily resolved. What's unique about James, and what makes it worthy of canonization, is its focus: It closely aligns with Jesus' own message. It is obvious from his manuscript that James was very familiar with Jesus' teachings, especially those found in the book of Matthew. For example, James (like Jesus) taught that the poor inherit God's kingdom, that the persecuted are blessed, and that merciful actions reflect faith. These references allow readers to infer that James thoroughly understood Jesus' message.

Also, James, like Jesus, was very much a *Jewish* Christian. He focused most of his attention on God the Father and who we are as God's creatures–favorite topics of Jewish believers. Unlike other New Testament writers, James assumed that his readers already knew and believed the gospel; now he wanted to make sure they fully understood the implications of living it out.

James let other people – such as the apostle Paul – worry about the theoretical details; James was more concerned with showing his readers how to live *practically* with Jesus. He wanted people to understand that yes, faith is certainly foundational, but it must be genuine, proven, and lived out if it's going to amount to anything.

a letter
from a friend

Lesson 1

If any of you lacks wisdom, he should ask God, who gives generously to all without finding fault, and it will be given to him.

James 1:5

When a friend writes you a letter, you might read it more than once (especially because he or she actually took the time to write a *letter*, not an e-mail). You read it first to get the general idea of what your friend is telling you. Maybe he's writing to tell you about new and exciting things in his life. Or maybe you haven't seen her in what seems like forever, and this letter reunites you. Then you might read it again to get the details. *What school is he going to? How many years has it been?* The second time around, you go over the details of the letter to really take in all your friend wants to tell you.

Like much of the New Testament, the book of James is actually a letter. Reading these letters is similar to reading a letter from a friend. But this letter was written nineteen hundred years before you were born; there are no juicy bits of personal information, and you aren't really that tight with its author. Other than that they're exactly the same. Seriously, it makes sense for us to look at James' letter as if it were written just for us, because it was, in a sense.

If you haven't already, read the introduction on page 13. This will introduce you to the book and show you how it fits with the rest of the Bible. Then read James' letter twice. First try reading a literal translation like the ESV (English Standard Version) or the NASB (New American Standard Bible). Then consider reading a paraphrase like *The Message*. That way, you will connect with both the *literal meaning* and the *feel* of the text.

1 As you read, write down your first impressions of the book. Consider the following questions, and take notes in the spaces below.

What kinds of themes show up? Do you notice one unifying topic throughout the book?

What is James' tone? Is he friendly, compassionate? Funny, dry?

What words does James repeat? (Repetition often clues us in to an author's focus.)

What kinds of language does James use? (Metaphors and pictures? Stories? Commands?)

2   Now that you have a good feel for James' letter, think up some alternative titles for the book, drawn from what you noticed. Write those here.

3   Try to infer James' purpose(s) for writing this letter. Explain your answer.

live

4   James wrote, "Do not merely listen to the word, and so deceive yourselves. Do what it says" (1:22). There's no question that reading and responding to God's Word will benefit our lives by drawing us nearer to Him – that's really what studying the Bible is all about. Did your overview of James suggest any areas of your life that you

want to work on during this study? If so, write them down here (or
in a private journal) and also note if you've already made plans to
deal with them. This is a time for you to come to God in confession
and praise, preparing yourself not only to study His Word, but also to
allow your life to be touched by James' letter.

5   After reading James all the way through, what are some questions you would like to have answered as you begin this in-depth
study?

connect

Upon receiving this letter from James, discuss with the group which part affects each of you the most. What sticks out to you, excites you, terrifies you, convicts you, and causes you to praise? Anything!

go deeper

For further study, read Psalm 119:97-104. How does James' attitude toward God's law compare to the one described in this passage? In light of what you've read, what is your attitude toward God's law?

memory verse of the week

Did a particular verse make you think? Is there a verse you can't get out of your head? Write it down and memorize it. Allow God's Word to permanently brand itself in your head and your heart.

notes from group discussion

notes from group discussion

when it gets tough

Consider it pure joy, my brothers, whenever you face trials of many kinds, because you know that the testing of your faith develops perseverance. Perseverance must finish its work so that you may be mature and complete, not lacking anything.

James 1:2-4

When James was alive, Jewish Christians were considered scandalous because they believed that a man who was executed as a criminal could actually be the Savior of the world. Here's a picture of what was going on: Christians were being persecuted—mostly by pagans whose power, money, self-esteem, and religious beliefs were challenged by Christian beliefs. Also, war was drawing near all over Judea. The Roman occupiers were cracking down on Jewish rebels, especially in Jerusalem. The Jews were livid.

In this section, James counsels Christians who are enduring the same struggles he is. Besides having to earn a living, pay taxes, raise families, and care for their health, they have all this persecution and war to deal with.

James isn't afraid to tell it like it is to his brothers and sisters; he gives them solid advice. Thousands of years later, his principles still help us handle life's many difficulties.

Read James 1:1-8, asking God to meet you in your everyday trials.

fyi

Twelve tribes (1:1). James wrote his letter to "the twelve tribes scattered among the nations." This refers to the Jewish Christians who were a part of the Dispersion (a time when God scattered His people throughout the earth because of their sin, but promised to eventually gather them together again and restore His nation). When Jesus came, the Jews thought that because He was the Messiah He would be the one to bring them together. But that's not how it went. Jesus said He would restore His earthly kingdom after He came to earth again. In the meantime, Christians are scattered all over to tell the world about God's love and to prepare themselves for a future with Jesus. So, when James says, "the twelve tribes scattered among the nations," he is referring figuratively to all Christians.

1   James gives us specific, not to mention challenging, guidelines for dealing with trials (1:2-4). How do you respond to them?

2   Read verses 3-4. These verses echo a theme often found elsewhere in Scripture; namely, life's trials actually help us live a complete life. Here are more verses to help you understand where James got his ideas. Write down what they say about trials and suffering.

Matthew 5:11-12

Romans 5:3-5

Hebrews 12:11

1 Peter 1:6-7

3   When we read this passage, it seems suffering is a major way in which God produces maturity and perseverance in us. Why do you think trials refine us so well?

fyi   ***Wisdom (1:5).*** In the book *How to Read the Bible for All Its Worth*, Gordon Fee and Douglas Stewart say wisdom is "the discipline of applying truth to one's life in the light of experience." Basically, this helps us understand that wisdom is not some up-in-the-clouds concept. Instead it's meant for down-to-earth living. It's also good to know that wisdom is a very popular topic in the Bible—three entire books are devoted to it: Proverbs, Job, and Ecclesiastes.

4   What does wisdom have to do with facing trials? Why should we pray for wisdom and not just perseverance?

5 In verses 5-8, James says God gives wisdom to anyone who asks. How does that compare with your experience?

6 James makes a big deal about not being double-minded, inconsistent, and unstable. Why do you think it's such an issue? What is the opposite of double-minded, and how does that help us understand?

live

7 God wants to help you get through trials and lead you to maturity. Describe a trial you're dealing with right now. During this next week, how can you trust Him to help?

8 Is there anything else you really responded to in this section? If so, write it down here.

connect

In your group, talk about some of the trials you are going through. Did anything James said help you? Do you still feel lost? Discuss honestly with each other the way you react to this lesson in the context of your daily life.

Then, because prayer is the foundation of authentic application, spend time praying together. Pray for each other, for wisdom and endurance in trials and for specific needs that anyone in your group may have. It's probably a good idea to thank God for the trials, considering we've spent this whole study learning about taking joy in our struggles.

go deeper

For further study, think and write about why faith is essential to receiving answers to prayer. See Mark 11:20-24 and Hebrews 11:6 for ideas.

memory verse of the week

Did a particular verse make you think? Is there a verse you can't get out of your head? Write it down and memorize it. Allow God's Word to permanently brand itself in your head and your heart.

notes from group discussion

tempting, but no thanks

Lesson 3

When tempted, no one should say, "God is tempting me." For God cannot be tempted by evil, nor does he tempt anyone.

James 1:13

In the previous lesson, James challenged us to take "pure joy" in struggles and to seek wisdom. In this next section, he focuses more on temptation. While the Greek meaning for *trial* and *temptation* is the same in these verses, James used them for entirely different purposes.

The difference comes in how James phrased his sentences. He was trying to show us that there is a distinction between *trials* that come from outward circumstances and *temptations* that come from our own hearts.

Reread James 1:1-8 to recap, and continue all the way through verse 18 for this lesson.

1 Context is always important when studying the Bible. It helps us understand the bigger picture, instead of only isolated statements. In the context of our reading for this lesson, explain where verses 5-8 and 9-11 fit.

5-8

9-11

2 What do you think James means when he refers to a "high position" and a "low position" (1:9,10)?

3 How can either of those positions potentially serve as a trial, something that leads to perseverance and maturity?

4 What does it mean to take pride in a "low position"? A "high position"? Explain the similarities and differences.

36

5 James gives a pretty compelling argument about why we should have joy through trials (1:2,12). Describe that argument in your own words.

6 How many times have we found ourselves saying things like "God put this temptation in my path" or "Satan's attack was the reason I sinned"? After reading verses 13-18, we can see that no one makes us sin but ourselves. From your reading on God's and our nature, how do we know it's impossible for God to tempt us to do evil? (If you want, also look at 1 John 1:5; 4:8-10.)

7 What is the real source of temptation to sin?

8   Explain the ultimate result of stepping toward temptation.

9   The truth of verse 15 is an unavoidable law – just as certain as the law of gravity. Think about the source of life. Why must desiring evil lead to death?

Firstfruits (1:18). Each year in Israel, the first bundle of harvested grain, the firstfruits, was offered to God as a sign that all of the grain in the field belonged to Him. This first bunch was the first in quality and in time, representing the whole of the field that would soon be gathered.

fyi

10   What do you think "He chose to give us birth through the word of truth" means (1:18)? Does it imply natural birth, spiritual rebirth, both, or something else?

11 Summarizing is an excellent study skill to practice. If you summarize a passage after you study it, you'll better understand its main point now and remember it later. Summarize the passage you read for this lesson (James 1:9-18).

live

Notice two alternate progressions of the life James has described:

>**Faith** – trials that test it – perseverance – maturity (1:2-4)
>**Desire** – temptation – sin – death (1:14-15)

We can move from tested faith to maturity or from indulged desire to death. Each process is a slow, almost unnoticeable series of choices we make daily. Choices lead to habits, and habits set a character either toward or against God.

12 God is the source of "every good and perfect gift" (1:17). What gifts can you ask for that would help you deal with temptation and make godly choices?

13 What's something that especially captured you in 1:9-18? Write about how you can grow in this area, what you can do this week to act on it, and how you can remember to follow through (be as specific as possible with your answers).

connect

Take time in your group to think about one temptation each of you has experienced recently. Think about the source of this temptation— was it something inward or something external? Reflect on this for a moment, then feel free to share (or not to share) with your group.

After this discussion, pray for each other. Praise God that He never changes and will always work in you through trials and temptations. Praise Him for giving you every good gift and never tempting you to do evil. Of course, pray for each other to make godly choices in your pursuit of a holy life.

go deeper

Look up 2 Timothy 2:22 and James 4:7-8 to further consider how to deal with evil desires. Write your thoughts and then memorize James 1:13-15.

memory verse of the week

Did a particular verse make you think? Is there a verse you can't get out of your head? Write it down and memorize it. Allow God's Word to permanently brand itself in your head and your heart.

notes from group discussion

notes from group discussion

real
religion

Lesson 4

Everyone should be quick to listen, slow to speak and slow to become angry, for man's anger does not bring about the righteous life that God desires.

James 1:19-20

So far, James has talked about trials and temptations. Now he hits hard on anger and gossip. But why did he make such a transition? What do anger and gossip have to do with temptation?

James has been talking theoretically thus far, but now he's getting to the heart of his message. Bringing in practical application, he challenges us to use the good and perfect gifts that God lavishes on us.

Read James 1:19-27 before moving on.

1   Why does James want us to be quick to listen and slow to speak (1:19)? What or who do you think he wants us to listen to?

2   How do talkativeness and a quick temper hinder a person from listening?

Humbly (1:21). Being humble helps us accept and obey what God says in His Word. When we're humble, we quickly seek help from God rather than trusting in our own abilities. In true humility, we don't have low self-esteem; we are just not overly occupied with ourselves. We don't have to worry about making ourselves first and shooting others down to gain approval. Some people think meekness and humility equal weakness. It's just not true, and Jesus is the perfect example. Jesus was humble—but He wasn't cowardly or incompetent. Instead He was courageous and bold. And, in humility, we can be too.

fyi

3   Summarize what James says about the Word in 1:18,21-22.

4 How is a person who hears without doing like one who looks in a mirror and later forgets what he or she sees (1:23-24)?

fyi **Religion (1:26-27).** Jews and Greeks had many specific definitions for what "pure" religion meant. To be truly religious, people had to be ceremonially clean (according to Moses' Law). They also had to perform acceptable service acts for God's temple. But James puts a new spin on this with his definition of pure religion. He rejects this idea of external purity and focuses on the heart and internal purity.

5 List some differences between worthless religion and pure religion.

Worthless religion	Pure religion

6 What does it mean to "keep oneself from being polluted by the world" (1:27)?

7   James wrote about looking intently into God's "perfect law that gives freedom" (1:25) and acting on it. Consider one significant command from this section and write about how you can act on it—and about how you can make sure you remember to do this.

Take time to think about one internal or external obstacle that keeps you from doing what God's Word says. And don't just call it "sin"; think specifically about what holds you back. Then, in the group, share those specific hurdles. (It will probably help everyone to know they're not alone, and people may discover practical ways to overcome those obstacles.) After your discussion, get in groups of two and pray for each other's specific obstacles, asking God to help you jump over them.

go deeper

We know that humility is important in understanding and applying God's Word. Study the following verses and explain in your own words what they say about humility.

Matthew 5:5

Galatians 5:23

Ephesians 4:2

2 Timothy 2:25

Titus 3:2

1 Peter 2:18

1 Peter 3:4,15

Describe situations, influences, and attitudes that make it difficult to be humble.

memory verse of the week

Did a particular verse make you think? Is there a verse you can't get out of your head? Write it down and memorize it. Allow God's Word to permanently brand itself in your head and your heart.

notes from group discussion

in-shape
Christianity

Lesson 5

If you really keep the royal law found in Scripture, "Love your neighbor as yourself," you are doing right.

James 2:8

James says that it's easy to spot the differences between lazy and active Christian lives. He says that when we're heading toward genuine spiritual maturity, we persevere while our faith is tested, we ask God for wisdom in trials, and above all, we listen to God's words and do what He says. James wants us to understand that while we *do* all these things to become spiritually mature, we can't do any of them without allowing God to help us.

Read James 2:1-13.

1   What three tests of true religion – active faith – did James list in 1:26-27? Of those three, which did James seem to focus on most in 2:1-13?

2   Where in your daily life do you interact with the poor? What do those interactions look like?

3   How does that differ from the way you interact with wealthy people?

4   It seems there's a practical comparison here to people we go to school with – the popular and unpopular. No matter which group you fit in, how can you treat everyone equally? Why does James suggest you do so?

fyi *Discriminated among yourselves (2:4).* The Greek word for *discrimination* means the same as doubt in 1:6. This word has the sense of wavering or being "divided." The Bible doesn't say we shouldn't recognize good from bad. Instead it suggests we choose the right things to discriminate against, like evil, and avoid judging unimportant issues like wealth or popularity.

5   What leads us to treat people who are rich/poor, popular/unpopular, smart/simple, and so on differently?

6   What's wrong with those motives, according to the royal law (2:8)?

7   Why does breaking one of God's laws make us guilty of breaking the whole thing (2:10-11)?

8   What are we saying about God when we break a law? (Optional: See Matthew 5:17-20,48; Romans 13:8-10.)

9 Is there someone in your life you discriminate against, judge, or reject? How can you treat that person with mercy instead?

10 This week, how can you begin to change your perspective about treating people of all socioeconomic statuses equally? (And don't just say, "Be nicer to people." Be specific.)

connect

Share how last week's efforts went as you sought to be doers of the Word. Do you have questions or need help, advice, or prayer? Which obstacles did you face? Where were you successful? Then discuss your reaction to this lesson in the context of what you learned last week. Do you feel encouraged? Discouraged? Both? Neither?

Get in groups of two and spend time in prayer. Praise Jesus for the way He treats all people, rich and poor. Pray that you would each learn to follow in His steps. Also, pray for each other's specific requests about applying this study.

Remember, it's okay if you didn't have overnight success. Maturity is an ongoing process; what God wants is our perseverance (1:2-4).

go deeper

Study how Jesus treated the poor, the working class, and the social rejects. Look up Luke 5:27-31; 14:12-14; and 15:1-7 for examples. Feel free to cross-reference these verses, or use your concordance to find more examples. Ask yourself, "How is this a model for me? How can I follow it?" Write your thoughts below.

memory verse of the week

Did a particular verse make you think? Is there a verse you can't get out of your head? Write it down and memorize it. Allow God's Word to permanently brand itself in your head and your heart.

notes from group discussion

notes from group discussion

faith and works, like hand in glove

Lesson 6

Suppose a brother or sister is without clothes and daily food. If one of you says to him, "Go, I wish you well; keep warm and well fed," but does nothing about his physical needs, what good is it? In the same way, faith by itself, if it is not accompanied by action, is dead.

James 2:15-17

Sometimes we know just the right "Christian" thing to say, don't we? We rattle off answers to difficult Bible questions, thinking we've got it down. Or we tell a suffering friend, "Don't worry. God will work it out" or "God won't give you more than you can handle!" We pray so articulately, say just the right words, pause in just the right places, use just the right tone of voice.

And sometimes we do all these things yet our lives don't reflect any of them. We don't seek the Scriptures to learn their depth, realizing there's no way we can know all the answers. When a friend comes to us desperate and in need, instead of offering help, we offer trite and useless words. Our prayers sound fancy, but they lack a humble heart.

In these verses, James discusses just how scary it is when our lives don't mesh with our words. He wants us to realize that a person not *living* for God is not alive at all, but a corpse.

Read James 2:14-26.

1 After reading 2:14-26, look at what else the Bible has to say about faith and works. Read the following passages and write down what Jesus, Paul, and John meant when they discussed active faith.

Jesus (Matthew 7:15-23; 25:31-46)

Paul (Galatians 5:6)

John (1 John 3:10,17-19)

2 Compare and contrast all four statements.

• *You have faith; I have deeds (2:18).* In this passage, James shows how some people twist Scripture. The person he objected to was probably referencing Paul's teachings on the different parts of the body and the different spiritual gifts. But James insisted (and Paul would agree) that every real Christian, regardless of his or her individual gifting, must have faith *and* works because works *demonstrate* faith.

• ***There is one God (2:19).*** This was and is the core of Jewish faith, recited daily in the form of what's called the *Shema,* found in Deuteronomy 6:4-5. Jesus quoted part of this creed as the greatest commandment in Matthew 22:37. Believing that there is only one God was the primary thing that set Christians apart from pagans. (But James says that "even the demons believe that—and shudder" [2:19]!) James explains that saying the right words (and even *believing* them) means nothing without action to support them.

3 James offers Abraham and Rahab as two examples of genuine faith. What did Abraham's willingness to sacrifice Isaac prove (see Genesis 22:12; James 2:22-24)?

4 How does what he did reflect what James wrote about faith in 1:2-4?

fyi   ***Righteous, justified (2:21,24-25).*** It's good to realize that the ways Paul and James spoke of "justification" are slightly different, because most people today use Paul's definition. For James, justification meant that salvation is demonstrated by the way we live out our faith. For Paul, we are justified the minute God saves us.

5 In *The Message*, James 2:18,22,26 reads, "Faith and works, works and faith, fit together hand in glove. . . . Isn't it obvious that faith and works are yoked partners, that faith expresses itself in works? . . . The very moment you separate body and spirit, you end up with a corpse. Separate faith and works and you get the same thing: a corpse."

In your own words, summarize the relationship between faith and works.

How does this compare to what you thought about faith and works before studying this passage?

live

6 Abraham showed faith by holding nothing back from God, not even his most valued treasure. Are you holding anything back from God? Is there anything you wouldn't give Him? Explain your answer.

7   Realizing that faith without action is dead, ask God to help you to do more than speak your surrender to Him – to live it! Write down a specific situation in which you can submit to God, and make an action plan on how to follow through.

connect

In your group, discuss why it's so difficult to submit our entire lives to God. Talk candidly with each other about the struggles to live out your beliefs in everyday life. Afterward pray silently and humbly before God. Ask God to help you demonstrate your faith by what you do, and ask Him to show you in which areas of your life He wants you to take action. Then pray as a group. Ask God to make you a community of people who will serve Him in surrender, desiring to show the world His love.

go deeper

Read the following passages. Does Paul agree or disagree with James? How do Paul's writings compare and contrast to James' letter?

Romans 13:8-10

Galatians 5:22-25

Philippians 2:12-13

memory verse of the week

Did a particular verse make you think? Is there a verse you can't get out of your head? Write it down and memorize it. Allow God's Word to permanently brand itself in your head and your heart.

notes from group discussion

the overflow of the heart

Lesson 7

With the tongue we praise our Lord and Father, and with it we curse men, who have been made in God's likeness. Out of the same mouth come praise and cursing. My brothers, this should not be.

James 3:9-10

It is so strange that a tiny part of our bodies, our tongues, can make such a difference in our pursuit of holiness. If we let ourselves, we can cause serious damage with our tongues. We gossip, curse people, spread lies, use biting sarcasm – all of which can harm others and ourselves.

In this passage, James wants us to realize that our mouths can be barriers to faithful living and that they are reflections of how active our faith really is. Jesus said, "Out of the overflow of the heart the mouth speaks" (Matthew 12:34).

James helps us understand just how dangerous our words can be, and he encourages us to seek God's help in taming the tongue.

Read James 3:1-12.

1   We know that teachers will be judged strictly (3:1). Why do you think that is? (Optional: Look at Matthew 12:33-37; Romans 2:17-24.)

2   How is a tongue like a horse's bit or a ship's rudder (3:2-5)?

3   In your own words, describe what James says about the tongue in 3:6.

4   Why is it especially horrible to curse or verbally abuse another person (3:9)?

5   Besides swearing, what other kinds of speech could verse 9 be referring to?

fyi **Perfect (3:2).** When we read that those who can control their
tongues are perfect, we may think, "I'm off the hook! After all,
nobody's perfect!" But excusing ourselves just because "nobody's perfect" is a mistake. The word *perfect* here is the same Greek word as
mature in 1:4 and *complete* in 2:22. According to Marvin R. Vincent
in his book *Word Studies in the New Testament*, it means "that which
has reached its maturity or fulfilled the end contemplated." The thing
is, God's goal for us *is* maturity and completeness. Although we
may never reach that goal in this life, we should always be growing
toward it.

6 James said it isn't possible for any human to attain perfection
in this life, but that we should seek it. How, then, can we control our
tongues and become mature? (Read Matthew 19:25-26 and James
1:5-8 for help.)

7   Many of us feel convicted when we read this part of James, because we struggle with getting our tongues under control. Looking at your own life and struggles, what can you do to become godlier in what you say? (Take a look at John 15:5-8; Romans 6:11-14; and James 4:6-10 for some guidance.)

8   Write down one specific thing you will do this week to help keep your tongue under control, and make a plan for how to accomplish this.

Think about the last loving thing you said. Also, think about the last hurtful thing you said. Do you recognize how people react differently when they are treated lovingly instead of hurtfully? How do you respond when you treat someone well rather than in a mean way? Discuss with each other some of your thoughts on how to control your tongue and avoid saying hurtful things.

Pray in your group about this coming week; pray that the Lord would help you meditate on the passage you studied tonight, remembering the potential damage the tongue can cause, but also remembering the potential goodness of kind words.

go deeper

In 3:6, James wrote that the tongue is "set on fire by hell." John also says that Satan is the "father of lies" (John 8:44). Does that mean that Satan is responsible for our evil words? Why, or why not? Read John 8:44 and feel free to look up other passages to support your argument.

memory verse of the week

Did a particular verse make you think? Is there a verse you can't get out of your head? Write it down and memorize it. Allow God's Word to permanently brand itself in your head and your heart.

notes from group discussion

notes from group discussion

becoming wise . . . on God's terms

Lesson 8

But the wisdom that comes from heaven is first of all pure; then peace-loving, considerate, submissive, full of mercy and good fruit, impartial and sincere.

James 3:17

We just read what James had to say about teachers: They should take their job seriously because they will be strictly judged. Well, we may not claim to be teachers, but we definitely offer plenty of advice to our friends (and anyone else who will listen).

We are often quick to speak into another's life. On the surface, there's nothing wrong with that—and there isn't if we are using God's wisdom. But when we start relying on our own "wisdom"—our amateur teaching methods—we'd better watch out so we aren't strictly judged.

Read James 3:13-18.

1   We know that a wise person is recognized by humble, good living. We also know that great leaders in the church, such as Jesus and Paul, taught with gentleness and humility. Why do you think humility and meekness are essential signs of wisdom?

2   Define in your own words the following from 3:14:

Bitter envy

Selfish ambition

3   In what ways do envy and selfish ambition lead to disorder and evil practices? (Optional: See Romans 1:18-32; Ephesians 4:17-19.)

78

4 How can they affect your relationships with God and others?

fyi **Disorder (3:16).** The word James used here suggests mental confusion. What's interesting about James' word choice is that mental confusion inevitably causes outward chaos and "every evil practice." It is the same word as *unstable* in 1:8. Basically, James is saying that earthly wisdom leads to the same inconsistent, wavering double-mindedness that he has been preaching against.

5 Contrast the effects of the wisdom that is "earthly, unspiritual, of the devil" (3:15-16) with those of the wisdom that comes from God (3:17-18).

"Earthly, unspiritual, of the devil"	Heavenly, spiritual, of God

6   James contrasted the maker of disorder – the Devil – to the maker of peace – God. After reading 3:13-18, what do you think it means to be a peacemaker?

7   How are peacemaking and righteousness related?

live

8   All of the good traits James discusses here come from "clothing" ourselves in heavenly wisdom and getting rid of worldly wisdom. Think about what you can do this week to wear heavenly wisdom (3:17-18).

What traits or habits do you need to confess and repent of?

What else can you do to grow in heavenly wisdom? Be as specific about your plans as possible.

connect

Are you a person who tends to give advice and counsel to others, or do you avoid that? Discuss this in your group. Talk about how you all can use godly wisdom in communication with each other. Then pray, thanking God for offering you His kind of wisdom. Ask Him to give each of you heavenly wisdom and the fruits that come with it.

go deeper

Look at your answer to question 5 in lesson 7. To think about this in more detail, consider Job 28:28; Psalm 119:9-16; Proverbs 8:12; Romans 8:5-8; and James 1:5-8.

memory verse of the week

Did a particular verse make you think? Is there a verse you can't get out of your head? Write it down and memorize it. Allow God's Word to permanently brand itself in your head and your heart.

notes from group discussion

notes from group discussion

what's your motivation?

Lesson 9

Submit yourselves, then, to God. Resist the devil, and he will flee from you. Come near to God and he will come near to you.

James 4:7-8

Having pure motives seems nearly impossible. Even when we're serving God, perhaps by helping the poor, our pride sneaks in and says, "People will think I'm *so* godly if I do this." And when we pray, we secretly want God to perform so we look good. *We have mixed motives.*

James wants to show us why the battle between our desire to serve God and our desire to serve ourselves constantly rages. As a result of this internal battle, we experience endless conflict in our lives and relationships. James knows the frustration of this tension, and he suggests we think differently about . . . well . . . ourselves.

Read James 4:1-10.

1 What do fighting and quarreling have to do with receiving things from God?

Adulterous people (4:4). In the Old Testament, God often describes Himself as the husband of His people, and the New Testament calls the church the bride of Christ. Because loving the world means hating God, to go after worldly pleasure is, truly, to cheat on God.

fyi

2 How does it affect you to know that God considers your pursuit of selfish goals to be adultery (4:4)?

World (4:4). So, what defines "the world" anyway? The Greek word used here, *kosmos,* can mean the physical universe, but more often it refers to humanity. In this context, James is suggesting that we have rebelled by seeking our significance and purpose in humanity, not in God—that we are easily led astray by Satan and need to be saved from ourselves.

fyi

3 From your experience and knowledge of Scripture, what are some symptoms of becoming too friendly with the world?

4   When James says that "the spirit he caused to live in us envies intensely," what does he mean (4:5)? And how does that fit into the context of this passage?

5   God offers abundant grace for us to overcome our cravings for pleasure, our envy, and our quarreling. Why does He only offer this grace if we are humble, and never if we are proud?

live

6   Notice that in verses 7-10 James used very active language. Clearly, humbling yourself and submitting to God is not a passive action. How can you actively submit to God today or tomorrow?

7   How can you transfer the things you've learned in this lesson about conflict and fighting to your everyday relationships?

8   What other questions or comments do you have about this passage?

connect

In your group, talk about recent fights or quarrels you've gotten into. What do you think caused them? Have someone in the group pray for grace and humility in the midst of conflict. Praise God for giving you instruction through James on the importance of humility. Thank Him for the grace He gives to the humble, and ask Him to help you submit to Him actively and to boldly resist the Devil and your own selfish pride.

go deeper

For more about resisting the Devil, see Matthew 4:1-11; Ephesians 6:10-18; 1 Peter 5:6-11; and 1 John 5:18.

memory verse of the week

Did a particular verse make you think? Is there a verse you can't get out of your head? Write it down and memorize it. Allow God's Word to permanently brand itself in your head and your heart.

notes from group discussion

notes from group discussion

opposition to the proud

Lesson 10

Anyone, then, who knows the good he ought to do and doesn't do it, sins.

James 4:17

James continues to hammer home his main point: We must live out our faith. In this passage, he quotes a timely proverb: "God opposes the proud." He then addresses three forms of pride, all of which we can relate to (unfortunately).

As James warns us about this worldly pride, he also provides reasons to be humble. He demonstrates the antidote to pride: heavenly wisdom that keeps us from being polluted by the world. To wrap up his argument, James shows us how each example of humility can be seen in the character of Christ Himself.

Read James 4:11–5:6.

Pride. There's good pride and bad pride. It's not bad to respect yourself, and it's okay to be satisfied in accomplishing something you've worked on diligently, such as standing firm in the midst of temptation or reaching a personal goal. Pride turns sour when it becomes self-absorbed and egotistical. That kind of pride moves our attention away from God and His power and instead shines the spotlight of praise on ourselves.

1   In 4:11-12, James discussed the first instrument of pride: our tongue. Why does speaking against a brother or sister mean that we're criticizing God's law?

2   Why is that prideful?

3   What attitude did James condemn in verses 13-14? How is this both proud and foolish?

4   It's not always wrong to make plans for our future (4:13). But how do we make future plans with humility?

5 Verse 17 seems to pop out of nowhere. Reread verses 13-16. How is verse 17 relevant, in context?

6 How does a rich person live humbly? Why is his or her situation unique (5:1-6)?

live

7 What warning, command, or truth from this section of Scripture most resonated with you? How do you need to grow in this area?

8   How do you plan to act on this truth and move toward growth?

connect

Discuss your answers to questions 7 and 8. Form groups of two or three and ask God to help you move toward growth. (It may be that people in your group fall into each of the three "pride camps." If that's the case, form groups based on which "camp" people fall into, so group members can pray with understanding for each other.)

go deeper

Whom are we acting like if we slander our brothers and sisters (see
Revelation 12:10)? What does Christ do instead (see 1 John 2:1-2)?
How can we apply this knowledge to our everyday lives?

memory verse of the week

Did a particular verse make you think? Is there a verse you can't get
out of your head? Write it down and memorize it. Allow God's Word
to permanently brand itself in your head and your heart.

notes from group discussion

notes from group discussion

while
I wait

Lesson 11

Therefore confess your sins to each other and pray for each other so that you may be healed. The prayer of a righteous man is powerful and effective.

James 5:16

There are times when we feel so deflated we just want to give up. Many people James wrote to – the poor and persecuted – felt that way. *Can I really go on? Jesus, where are You? Why haven't You come back yet?*

In this section of his letter, James says, "Don't give up!" He encourages his friends to persevere, to press on (as he did in chapter 1), and to keep hoping for a triumphant future with Jesus.

Read James 5:7-20.

1   You can't understand verses 7-12 without remembering the context of verses 1-6. Reread these verses. Explain how the two passages challenge us to be patient.

Near (5:8). Two thousand years seems like a long time to us, but in God's perspective, it's no time at all. So, in that sense, Christ's return is still very "near." But God's kingdom is also here and now—today—because Christ has made it possible for us to have a personal relationship with the Father.

fyi

2   Knowing we've been waiting for two thousand years, what are your thoughts when you consider Jesus' second coming is still "near"?

3   You probably know a little about Job's persecution story. But did you know that almost every prophet of the Old Testament suffered great persecution? Do you agree that those who suffer are blessed (5:10-11)? Why, or why not? (Optional: To learn about some of the blessings that come from perseverance, see Matthew 5:10-12; 10:28-31; James 1:12; Revelation 2:7,11,26-28; 3:5,12,21.)

4   James warns his readers against swearing. Not the kind of swearing you hear in movies – or perhaps coming from your own mouth on occasion. This type of swearing involves making promises we won't or can't keep. Why is breaking your word so offensive to God? (For help on this, read Exodus 20:7 and Matthew 5:33-37.)

5   James counsels his readers to live patiently. Write down *what* he advises in each of these circumstances and *why* these might be wise actions.

If we are in trouble

If we are happy

If we are sick

6   The Greek word James uses for "healing" means physical, psychological, *and* spiritual healing. From what we read in 5:15, explain in your own words the two factors that bring about this healing.

7   Who in the body of believers has the responsibility to take action if a brother or sister is wandering (5:19)?

8   We also know that only God can save a sinner. What does James mean when he says that one of us should bring the wanderer back?

live

9   Describe a time when you said you would or wouldn't do something and didn't follow through.

10   What can you do this week to be more consistent in keeping your word?

connect

Because the last part of James' letter is all about confessing to and praying for each other, spend time discussing your personal needs. Pray for one another. Remember that hearing each other's confessions and prayers is part of being in the family of God. None of us is in any position to judge, so don't be judgmental. If you must, ask God to help you be humble.

go deeper

In what ways have you suffered for your faith? According to the following verses, how should you react to suffering?

Luke 18:1

Luke 22:39-44

2 Corinthians 12:7-10

1 Peter 5:10

memory verse of the week

Did a particular verse make you think? Is there a verse you can't get out of your head? Write it down and memorize it. Allow God's Word to permanently brand itself in your head and your heart.

notes from group discussion

follow through

Lesson 12

Do not merely listen to the word, and so deceive yourselves. Do what it says. Anyone who listens to the word but does not do what it says is like a man who looks at his face in a mirror and, after looking at himself, goes away and immediately forgets what he looks like.

James 1:22-24

James doesn't want us just to read the Bible. He wants it to change our lives. That's why again and again James encourages us to do what we know we are supposed to do. *Hear, do. Hear, do. Hear, do.* It's a perfect picture of what faith in action looks like.

Wrap up your study by reviewing why good intentions just aren't good enough—why we need to take that next step. Just like in basketball, it's all about follow-through.

Here are some questions to help you thoroughly review the book. Have fun. As you finish, pray that God will help you to be a doer of His Word.

1 Reread James' entire letter. It should be fairly familiar to you by now, so it will go quickly. As you read, look for common threads that tie the book together. Ask God to help you read with a fresh perspective. Record some of your observations.

2 Summarize James' teachings on these topics:

Trials (1:2-12; 5:7-16)

Temptations (1:13-18; 4:1-12; 5:19-20)

Prayer (1:5-8; 4:1-3; 5:13-18)

The tongue (3:1-12; 4:1-3,11-12; 5:9,12)

Wisdom (1:5-8; 3:13-18)

Wealth and poverty (1:9-11,27; 2:1-9; 5:1-6)

Faith and deeds (1:22-27; 2:14-26; 3:13)

Single-mindedness and double-mindedness
(1:5-8,14,22-24; 2:4; 3:9-12,16-18; 4:1-10; 5:12)

Any other major topics

live

Because we've been talking about being "doers," let's take a look at
how we're doing. The point of this exercise is not to condemn ourselves because we aren't measuring up, but instead to confess, be
encouraged, and grow.

3   Think about the primary truths you wanted to apply to your life as you've studied the book of James. Ask yourself the questions below – and answer honestly. What can you learn from this that will help you mature as a Christian?

Am I becoming more and more patient in trials?

Am I learning to resist temptation from the start instead of playing with it?

Am I learning to find joy in obeying the Word of God?

Are there any prejudices that shackle me?

Am I learning to control my tongue?

Am I a friend of God or a friend of the world?

Do I make plans without considering God's will?

Am I naturally depending on prayer when I find myself in trouble?

What is my attitude toward a brother or sister who is wandering from the faith? Do I criticize or gossip, or do I seek to restore him or her in love?

4   Look back through the study and note your plans to grow. Are you satisfied with your follow-through? Where do you still feel challenged? Use the space below to make plans to continue applying what you learned in James.

connect

Spend time evaluating your group dynamics during this study of James. What did you like best about your meetings? What did you like least, and what would you change? How did you grow and become more unified as a group? Talk about how studying James changed you, as a group and individually. Then thank God together for what He has taught you, how He has changed you, and how He will continue to work through you as you seek to "not merely listen to the word . . . [but] do what it says" (1:22).

go deeper

Write down what James says about the nature of God in each of the following passages. Describe at least one implication each statement has for your life.

	God's nature	Implication
1:5		
1:13		
1:17		
1:20		
1:27		

	God's nature	Implication
2:5		
4:6		
4:12		
5:11		

Now write down what James says about human nature, and again, what those statements imply to us.

	Human nature	Implications
1:18		

	Human nature	Implications
3:9		
4:14		

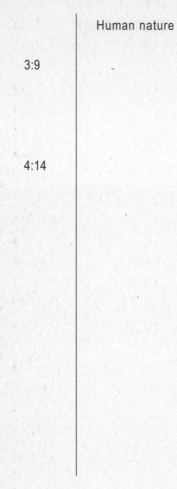

memory verse of the week

Did a particular verse make you think? Is there a verse you can't get out of your head? Write it down and memorize it. Allow God's Word to permanently brand itself in your head and your heart.

notes from group discussion

study resources

It's true that studying the Bible can often lead you to answers for life's tough questions. But Bible study also prompts plenty of *new* questions. Perhaps you're intrigued by a passage and want to understand it better. Maybe you're stumped about what a particular verse or word means. Where do you go from here? Study resources can help. Research a verse's history, cultural context, and connotations. Look up unfamiliar words. Track down related Scripture passages elsewhere in the Bible. Study resources can help sharpen your knowledge of God's Word.

Below you'll find a selected bibliography of study resources. Use them to discover more, dig deeper, and ultimately grow closer to God.

historical and background sources

D. A. Carson, Douglas Moo, and Leon Morris. *An Introduction to the New Testament.* Grand Rapids, MI: Zondervan, 1992.

Provides an overview of the New Testament for students and teachers. Covers historical and biographical information and includes outlines and discussions of each book's theological importance.

James I. Packer, Merrill C. Tenney, and William White Jr. *The Bible Almanac.* Nashville: Thomas Nelson, 1980.

Contains information about people of the Bible and how they lived. Photos and illustrations help the characters come to life.

Merrill C. Tenney. *New Testament Survey.* Grand Rapids, MI: Eerdmans, 1985.

Analyzes social, political, cultural, economic, and religious backgrounds of each New Testament book.

concordances, dictionaries, and atlases

concordances

If you are studying a specific word and want to know where to find it in the Bible, use a concordance. A concordance lists every verse in the Bible in which that word shows up. An *exhaustive* concordance includes every word in a given translation (there are different concordances for different Bible translations) and an *abridged* or *complete* concordance leaves out some words, some occurrences of the words, or both. Multiple varieties exist, so choose for yourself which one you like best. *Strong's Exhaustive Concordance* and *Young's Analytical Concordance of the Bible* are the most popular.

Bible dictionaries

Sometimes called a *Bible encyclopedia,* a Bible dictionary alphabetically lists articles about people, places, doctrines, important words, customs, and geography of the Bible. Here are a few to consider:

Nelson's New Illustrated Bible Dictionary. Nashville: Thomas Nelson, 1996.
> *Includes over 500 photos, maps, and pronunciation guides.*

The New Strong's Expanded Dictionary of Bible Words. Nashville: Thomas Nelson, 2001.
> *Defines more than 14,000 words. In addition, it includes an index that gives meanings of the word in the original language.*

The New Unger's Bible Dictionary. Wheaton, IL: Moody, 1988.
> *Displays pictures, maps, and illustrations. Clearly written, easy to understand, and compatible with most Bible translations.*

Vine's Expository Dictionary of New Testament Words. Peabody, MA: Hendrickson, 1993.
> *Lists major words and defines each New Testament Greek word.*

Bible atlases

We often skim over mentions of specific locations in the Bible, but location is an important element to understanding the context of a passage. A Bible atlas can help you understand the geography in a book of the Bible and how it may have affected the recorded events. Here are two good choices:

The Carta Bible Atlas. Jerusalem: Carta, 2003.
> *Includes analytical notes on biblical events, military campaigns, travel routes, archeological highlights, as well as indexes. A very popular atlas for students, scholars, and clergy.*

The Illustrated Bible Atlas. Grand Rapids, MI: Kregel, 1999.
> *Provides concise (and colorful) information on lands and cities where events took place. Includes historical notes.*

for small-group leaders

If you are the leader of a small group or would like to lead a small group, these resources may help.

Ann Beyerlein. *Small Group Leaders' Handbook.* Downer's Grove, IL: InterVarsity, 1995.
> *Teaches the biblical basis and growth stages of small groups. Helps leaders develop skills for resolving conflict, leading discussion, and planning for the future.*

Neal F. McBride. *How to Lead Small Groups.* Colorado Springs, CO: NavPress, 1990.
> *Covers leadership skills for all kinds of small groups. Filled with step-by-step guidance and practical exercises focusing on the most important aspects of small-group leadership.*

Laurie Polich. *Help! I'm a Small-Group Leader.* Grand Rapids, MI: Zondervan, 1998.

> *Offers tips and solutions to help you nurture your small group and accomplish your goals. Suggests techniques and questions to use in many Bible study circumstances.*

Bible study methods

Gordon Fee and Douglas Stuart. *How to Read the Bible for All Its Worth.* Grand Rapids, MI: Zondervan, 2003.

> *Offers chapters on interpreting and applying the different kinds of writing in the Bible: Epistles, Gospels, Old Testament Law, Old Testament narrative, the Prophets, Psalms, Wisdom, and Revelation. Also includes suggestions for commentaries on each book of the Bible.*

Tim LaHaye. *How to Study the Bible for Yourself.* Eugene, OR: Harvest House, 1998.

> *Teaches how to illuminate Scripture through study. Gives methods for understanding the Bible's major principles, promises, commands, key verses, and themes.*

Oletta Wald. *The New Joy of Discovery in Bible Study.* Minneapolis: Augsburg, 2002.

> *Helps students of Scripture discover how to observe all that is in a text, how to ask questions of a text, and how to use grammar and passage structure to see the writer's point. Teaches methods for independent Bible study.*

BULK PRICING
Is Available

Order enough for everyone in your group!

For more information on all NavPress products or to find additional Bible studies, go to **www.NavPress.com** or call **1-800-366-7788**.

NAVPRESS
Discipleship Inside Out®